W9-BXT-428

AMAZING
Primates

Gibbons

Written by
Anita Yasuda

www.av2books.com

AV^2 provides enriched content that supplements and complements this book. Weigl's AV^2 books strive to create inspired learning and engage young minds in a total learning experience.

Your AV^2 Media Enhanced books come alive with...

Go to **www.av2books.com**, and enter this book's unique code.

BOOK CODE

H722232

AV^2 by Weigl brings you media enhanced books that support active learning.

Audio
Listen to sections of the book read aloud.

Video
Watch informative video clips.

Embedded Weblinks
Gain additional information for research.

Try This!
Complete activities and hands-on experiments.

Key Words
Study vocabulary, and complete a matching word activity.

Quizzes
Test your knowledge.

Slide Show
View images and captions, and prepare a presentation.

... and much, much more!

Published by AV^2 by Weigl
350 5th Avenue, 59th Floor
New York, NY 10118
Websites: www.av2books.com   www.weigl.com

Library of Congress Cataloging-in-Publication Data

Yasuda, Anita.
Gibbons / Anita Yasuda.
     pages cm. -- (Amazing primates)
Includes bibliographical references and index.
ISBN 978-1-4896-2874-9 (hard cover : alk. paper) -- ISBN 978-1-4896-2875-6 (soft cover : alk. paper) --
ISBN 978-1-4896-2876-3 (single user ebook) -- ISBN 978-1-4896-2877-0 (multi-user ebook)
1. Gibbons--Juvenile literature. I. Title.
 QL737.P943Y37 2014
 599.88'2--dc23
                              2014038982

Printed in the United States of America in Brainerd, Minnesota
1 2 3 4 5 6 7 8 9 0 18 17 16 15 14

122014
WEP081214

Project Coordinator: Katie Gillespie
Art Director: Terry Paulhus

Contents

Meet the Gibbon

Gibbons are **mammals** that belong to the **order** of **primates**. They are the smallest of the apes. Like all apes, gibbons have no tail.

Gibbons are arboreal, which means that they live in trees. They spend nearly all of their lives high above the ground in their forest **habitat**. Gibbons are the fastest of the apes. They can swing through the trees at a speed of 35 miles (56 kilometers) per hour.

While most apes feed on plants and meat, gibbons are **frugivores**. Their small size allows them to move along thin branches and to reach fruit that larger animals cannot. Gibbons live in family groups. Known as the singing apes, gibbons produce complex vocalizations that are quite musical.

The gibbon is skilled at swinging through forests as if it were flying. Gibbons can move 20 feet (6 meters) in a single swing.

Log on to www.av2books.com

AV² by Weigl brings you media enhanced books that support active learning. Go to www.av2books.com, and enter the special code found on page 2 of this book. You will gain access to enriched and enhanced content that supplements and complements this book. Content includes video, audio, weblinks, quizzes, a slide show, and activities.

AV² Online Navigation

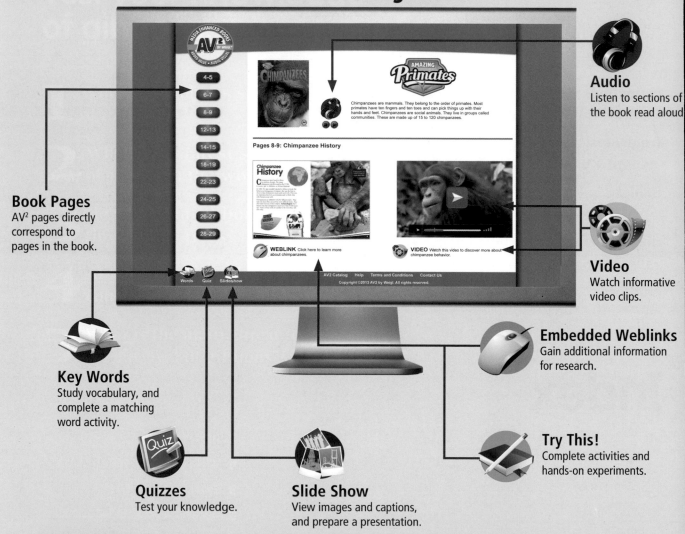

Audio
Listen to sections of the book read aloud.

Book Pages
AV² pages directly correspond to pages in the book.

Video
Watch informative video clips.

Key Words
Study vocabulary, and complete a matching word activity.

Embedded Weblinks
Gain additional information for research.

Quizzes
Test your knowledge.

Slide Show
View images and captions, and prepare a presentation.

Try This!
Complete activities and hands-on experiments.

AV² was built to bridge the gap between print and digital. We encourage you to tell us what you like and what you want to see in the future.

Sign up to be an AV² Ambassador at www.av2books.com/ambassador.

Due to the dynamic nature of the Internet, some of the URLs and activities provided as part of AV² by Weigl may have changed or ceased to exist. AV² by Weigl accepts no responsibility for any such changes. All media enhanced books are regularly monitored to update addresses and sites in a timely manner. Contact AV² by Weigl at 1-866-649-3445 or av2books@weigl.com with any questions, comments, or feedback.

24